This book belongs to:

_____

From:

_____

Bedtime Blessings for Boys

Carolyn Larsen

Illustrated by Caron Turk

christian
art kids

Copyright © 2009 by Christian Art Kids, an imprint of Christian Art Publishers,
PO Box 1599, Vereeniging, 1930, RSA

1025 N Lombard Road, Lombard, IL, 60148, USA

First edition 2009

Developed in co-operation with Educational Publishing Concepts.

Text copyright © 2009 by Carolyn Larsen
Art copyright © 2009 by Caron Turk
All rights reserved.

Cover designed by Christian Art Kids

Scripture quotations are taken from the *Holy Bible*, New Century Version®, NCV®,
copyright © 1987, 1988, 1991 by Word Publishing, a division of Thomas Nelson, Inc.
Used by permission.

Printed in China

ISBN 978-1-77036-098-3

11 12 13 14 15 16 17 18 19 20 – 14 13 12 11 10 9 8 7 6 5

Contents

Dear Parents,

What's your family's bedtime routine?

Snuggling, reading and praying together with freshly bathed little ones are such special times when your children are small. Then there's the joy of peeking into their rooms and watching them sleep peacefully. What a delight!

Sending your children to bed with comforting thoughts of God's personal love and care for them certainly can help with that peaceful sleep. It is our hope that these gentle stories of God's generous blessings will help your children learn how much God cares for them and send them to bed with warm and comforting thoughts.

Enjoy these years of snuggling, reading and praying ... they go so fast, so, make a lot of memories!

Blessings,

Carolyn and Caron

God Made Everything!

God looked at everything He had made,
and it was very good.
Genesis 1:31

God made everything,
everything there is!
God made big, juicy caterpillars
and squishy, squashy jellyfish.
God made long and shiny snakes,
and ants that are tiny.
God made pebbles to skip
across a pond.
God made everything,
everything there is!

God made mountains with snow on the top.
God made deep, deep oceans filled with
fish, whales and octopuses.

God made the moon and stars to
light the dark night.
God made the warm sun
for daytime.
God made everything,
everything there is.
And best of all ...
God made you!

Sweet Thoughts
to Sleep On

God made trees for you to climb. He made families to love you and friends to enjoy. God made everything!

★ What is your favorite animal that God made?

Dear God,

I love the world You made.
You did an awesome job!
Thank You for making everything!

Amen.

God Is Your Helper

The LORD is with me to help me.
Psalm 118:7

Have you ever thought you don't need any help?
No help at all?
Have you discovered that you sometimes DO need help?

Who will help you?
God will!
He will help you to work hard.
He will help you to obey.
He will help you to be brave and courageous.

He will help you be helpful and kind to others.
God wants to be your helper!

Sweet Thoughts
to Sleep On

Just because you need help sometimes doesn't mean you aren't a big boy. Everyone needs help sometimes. God wants to be your helper. Just ask Him for whatever you need!

★ How has God helped you?

Dear Father,

Thank You for helping me all the time.
Thank You for helping me to be kind
and helpful to others too.

Amen.

God Loves You

God is love. Those who live in love
live in God, and God lives in them.
1 John 4:16

God loves you, did you know that?
Yes, He does and He shows you every day!
How can you know that God loves you?
Look around ... He made ponds that
you can skim rocks over.

His love shows in the great family He gave you.
God gives you daytime for playing with your friends.
He gives you night-time for sleeping.
He makes your muscles rest at night-time.

God made trees and clouds and puppies
and kittens for you to enjoy!
God shows you every day
that He really loves you.

Sweet Thoughts
to Sleep On

Every day God shows how much He loves you. He gives you things you need like food and water. He gives you special treats like wiggly worms and snow to play in. God likes to give you special things because He loves you so much.

★ What is your favorite way that God shows He loves you?

Dear Father,

The Bible tells me that You love me.
Thanks for showing me that
You do — every day.

Amen.

God Protects You

The LORD will keep you safe.
Proverbs 3:26

Are you glad to have someone to take care of you every day?
Who are some people who take care of you?
Your mom and dad take care of you.
They make sure you have healthy food.
They make sure you have a home and a bed to sleep in.
They teach you rules to obey that will keep you safe.

Did you know that God protects you, too? He does!
He watches over you when you're playing soccer.

He protects you when you're climbing a tree.
He watches over you when you're snuggled in bed.
God protects you because He loves you!

Sweet Thoughts
to Sleep On

You can sleep well tonight because God is
watching over you. There is nothing for
you to worry about. Nothing will happen
that God doesn't know about.

★ How does God take care of you each day?

Dear Father,

Thank You for taking care of me.
I'm glad to know that You are
always watching over me.

Amen.

Obeying God

You must obey the LORD your God
and do what He says is right.
Exodus 15:26

Obey. Obey. Obey. Do you get tired
of being told you must obey?
Did you know that there are laws and
rules everyone must obey?
How do you learn to obey?
You learn how to obey God
by reading the Bible.

BIBLE

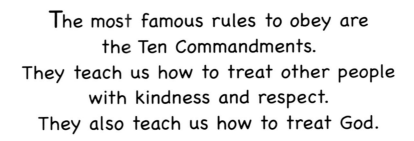

The most famous rules to obey are
the Ten Commandments.
They teach us how to treat other people
with kindness and respect.
They also teach us how to treat God.

1. Worship only God.
2. Do not worship idols.
3. Do not use God's name as a swear word.
4. Keep the Sabbath holy.
5. Honor your Father and Mother.

6. Do not murder.
7. Keep your marriage pure.
8. Do not steal.
9. Do not lie.
10. Do not want things that belong to others.

Jesus said that the most important thing is to love God.
Loving other people by showing kindness
is the next most important rule.
Jesus said that so you know it is true!

Sweet Thoughts
to Sleep On

Loving God and others is obeying God.
Obeying equals love!

★ Is obeying hard for you? Why?

Dear Father,

Obeying isn't always easy.
But I want to show You that I love You.
So please help me to obey!

Amen.

Loving God

Love the LORD your God with all your heart,
all your soul, and all your strength.
Deuteronomy 6:5

How do you tell God that you love Him?
Do you run and jump and celebrate?
Do you sing a loud, happy song?
Maybe you draw a picture of your favorite
thing He made. It doesn't matter how you
tell Him — just as long as you tell Him.

Why do you love God so much?
Do you love Him for taking care
of you in the dark night?

Do you love Him for making the
sun to light the daytime?
Do you love Him for giving you a
family and friends to enjoy?
You love Him for all
these things and more! So ... tell Him!

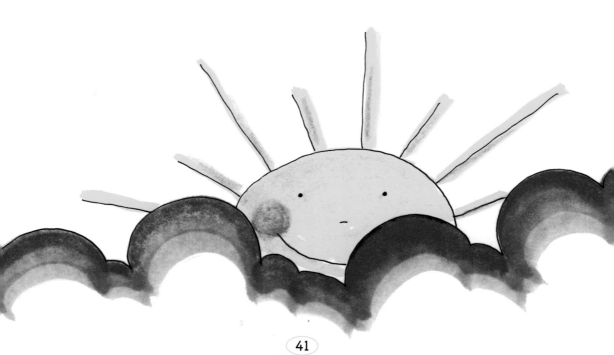

Sweet Thoughts
to Sleep On

There are many reasons to love God.
Remember to tell Him every day that you love Him.

★ What's your favorite way to show
God how much you love Him?

Dear Father,

Thank You for giving me so much. I really love
You and I want to show You every day.

Amen.

Showing Love to Others

"Love each other."
John 13:34

Some people are easy to love. But some are not.
Some people are mean and they don't play fair.
Some people are selfish and say unkind things.
These people are not easy to love.
Being kind. Saying nice things. Helping. Obeying and sharing.
These are ways of showing love to others.

People who are easy to love are friendly and kind.
They always share. That's much nicer!
Jesus showed love to everyone,
especially to those who were not easy to love.

He said that anyone can love their friends.
That's easy.
Only someone who loves God can love
people who aren't nice. That's harder.
Loving others shows we love God!

Sweet Thoughts
to Sleep On

God loves you — no matter what!
He said you should love other people too.
That means even people who may not be nice to you.

★ Name someone who is easy to love.

Bible

Dear Father,

Some people are hard for me to love.
Please help me to love them.

Amen.

God Is Always With You

God has said, "I will never leave you;
I will never abandon you."
Hebrews 13:5

When you pull the covers up and fall asleep,
God is with you.
When your eyes pop open and a new day begins,
God is with you.
When you are running down the soccer field,
God is with you.
When you are climbing the jungle gym,
God is with you.

When the sun is shining and birds are singing,
God is with you.
When thunder is booming and lightning is flashing,
God is with you.
God is with you when you are all alone,
and when you are with your friends.
God is with you when you are
eating lunch with your family.

God is with you when you are yahoo-happy,
and when you are shhh-quiet.
God is with you all the time,
every minute of every day and every night ...
Because He loves you very much!

Sweet Thoughts
to Sleep On

You are never ever alone.
God is with you all the time because
He loves you very much.

★ What's your favorite time to know
that God is with you?

Dear Father,

I don't like to be alone.
I'm glad to know that You are ALWAYS with me!

Amen.

God Sent Jesus

A child has been born to us;
God has given a son to us.

Isaiah 9:6

Do you like to get presents? Sure you do — it's fun!
God gave you a really special gift.
He sent His Son, Jesus, to earth.
Jesus taught that it's important to obey God.

Some people didn't like what Jesus taught.
They put Him on a wooden cross where He died.
But God brought Jesus back to life!

God sent Jesus to earth because He loves you.
God wants you to live in heaven with Him someday.
You can — because of what Jesus did.
Jesus was a really special gift, wasn't He?

Sweet Thoughts
to Sleep On

There's proof that God loves you very much —
He sent His very own Son to earth for you!

★ Do you understand how special God's gift of Jesus is?

Dear Father,

Thank You for loving me so much.
Thank You for sending Jesus.

Amen.

God Comforts You

God is the Father who is full of mercy and all comfort.
He comforts us every time we have trouble.

2 Corinthians 1:3-4

Have you ever had a very sad, not-so-good,
nothing-goes-right kind of day?
That's the kind of day when your
friends won't play with you!
On a nothing-goes-right kind of day you
get in trouble for picking on your sister,
your puppy runs away, you strike out in
baseball ... it's a very sad, not-so-good,
nothing-goes-right kind of day!

What will make you feel better?
Who can help?
There is Someone who loves you very
much. He will help you!
It's God! He loves you more
than anyone else!

64

He will help your very sad, not-so-good,
nothing-goes-right kind of day turn right around!
How does He do that? He helps you
remember how much He loves you.
He helps you remember that His
strength is there when you need it.
He loves you, plain and simple.

Sweet Thoughts
to Sleep On

Sometimes the best way to get through a hard day is to think about happy things. So, think about how MUCH God loves you.

★ When have you had a very sad, not-so-good, nothing-goes-right kind of day?

Dear Father,

Thank You for caring about my very sad, not-so-good, nothing-goes-right kind of day. Thank You for reminding me that You love me!

Amen.

Talking to God

"When you pray, you should pray like this:
'Our Father in heaven, may Your name always be kept holy.'"
Matthew 6:9

Talking with God is called prayer.
God wants to know when you are happy.
He wants to know when you are sad.
He wants to know that you love Him.

You learn what other people are
thinking when you talk with them.
Other people learn what you are
thinking by talking with you.
You talk to your friends about
things you like to do.

You talk to your mom and dad about what
you want to be when you grow up.
You talk with lots of people every day –
don't forget to talk to God too!

Sweet Thoughts to Sleep On

God wants to know what's on your mind.
He cares. Talk to Him whenever you want.

★ What would you like to tell God?

Dear God,

I'm glad I can talk with You.
Thank You for hearing
my prayers. Thank You for
loving me so much.

Amen.

Being Kind

Be kind and loving to each other,
and forgive each other.
Ephesians 4:32

Jesus said, "Treat other people the
way you would like to be treated."
What does that mean?
Speak kind words.
Don't shout at others.
Don't say mean things.

Share your stuff.
Let your brother or sister
go first sometimes.
That is being kind.

Pick up your toys and put them away.
Jesus said that being kind to others means
they will want to be kind to you.
That makes everyone feel happy!

Sweet Thoughts
to Sleep On

Jesus treated others with kindness.
So when you are kind, you are being like Jesus!

★ How can you show kindness to someone?

Dear Father,

Help me to be kind, even when I'm grumpy and tired. I want to be like Jesus.

Amen.

Being Patient

Always be patient.
Ephesians 4:2

Some friends cheat at games.
Some friends always want to go first.
Some friends want to play with your favorite toy.
Some friends always want to have their own way.
Some friends are not very patient.

Being patient means that you don't get
mad — even when your friend gets mad.
It means you are kind when your friend
wants to play baseball and you want to play soccer.
Being patient means thinking about
others instead of yourself.

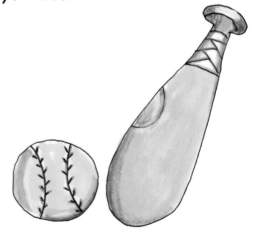

Some people are patient with you
when you are selfish, aren't they?
The most patient of all is God!
God is patient with you because He loves you.

Sweet Thoughts
to Sleep On

God is patient with you because He loves you.
You can show God's love to others
by being patient with them.

★ When has God been patient with you?

Mine!

Dear Father,

I know that I am selfish sometimes and sometimes I am grumpy. Thank You for being patient with me. Help me to be patient with others.

Amen.

Praying for Others

Always pray for all God's people.
Ephesians 6:18

Your friend is sad because his puppy ran away,
what can you do?
Your grandma is lonely, what can you do?
Your sister is scared of thunderstorms, what can you do?
If someone you love is sick, what can you do?

You can't make a sick person well.
You can't always make a sad person happy.

But there is something you can do ...
something really special!
You can pray for your friend or loved one.
Praying is asking God to help. He wants you
to ask because He wants to help!

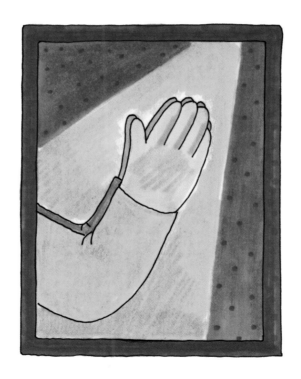

God loves your friend or family member
even more than you do.
Praying for others is the absolute
best thing you can do!

Sweet Thoughts
to Sleep On

Pray for ...

Praying for others is the best way to help ...
whatever their problems may be! God wants
to help because He loves them too.

★ Who could you pray for right now?

Dear Father,

I'm glad I can pray for others. It's the best way to help them. Thank You for loving my family and friends even more than I do!

Amen.

Helping Others

Be ready to do good.
Titus 3:1

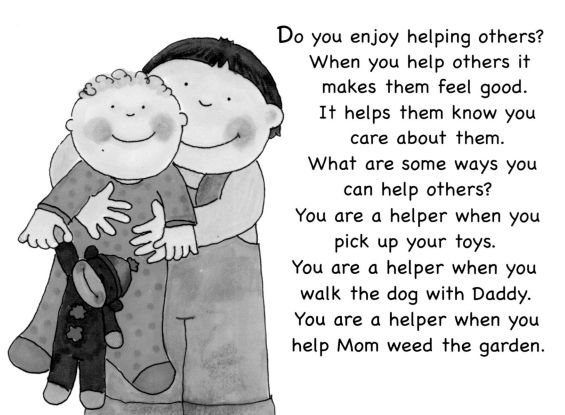

Do you enjoy helping others?
When you help others it
makes them feel good.
It helps them know you
care about them.
What are some ways you
can help others?
You are a helper when you
pick up your toys.
You are a helper when you
walk the dog with Daddy.
You are a helper when you
help Mom weed the garden.

You are a helper when you write
a letter to Grandma and Grandpa.
When you help others you
are being like Jesus.

Dear Grandma
and Grandpa

I Love You!

Jesus helped people when they were sad or sick.
Jesus helped everyone He could.
Jesus is happy when you are a helper too!

Sweet Thoughts
to Sleep On

Helping others is a nice thing to do.
Helping others shows that I love them!

★ How can you be a helper to someone?

Dear Father,

Please help me to think of ways to be a helper.
Thank You for all the people who help me!

Amen.

1. Walk the dog
2. Clean my room
3. Feed the dog
4. Help Mommy
5. Put toys away

God Gives You
All You Need

God will use His wonderful riches in Christ Jesus
to give you everything you need.
Philippians 4:19

God knows what you need to live each day.
He gives you everything you need!
You need good food to grow
strong, healthy muscles.
God gives it!
You need drinking water to
keep your body running well.
God gives that too.

Your mommy and daddy who take
care of you are a gift from God.
The friends you play in the sandbox
with are gifts from God.

Bright, warm sunlight is a gift from God.
The night-time moon and twinkling
stars are gifts from God.
God gives you EVERYTHING you need!

Sweet Thoughts
to Sleep On

God knows what you need each day. The cool thing is that sometimes He gives you things you don't really need. He gives them just so you can enjoy them.

★ What's your favorite thing God has given you?

Dear God,

Thanks for giving me things.
It shows me that
You think about me lots!
I think about You too!

Amen.

God Forgives You

If we confess our sins, He will forgive our sins,
because we can trust God to do what is right.

1 John 1:9

Everyone does wrong things sometimes.
Even grown-ups!
Sometimes we fight and
argue with friends.
This hurts God because
it breaks His rules about
how to treat others.

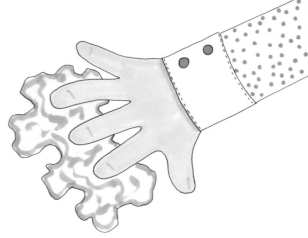

Wrong things are called sin.
God is sad when we sin.
But He doesn't get angry.
Do you know what He does?
He forgives.

Yes! He will give you a second chance
to be kind and considerate.
He gives second chances and third chances;
even a bazillion chances!
Do you know why He does that?
Because He LOVES YOU!

God knows that the more chances you get to obey,
the more you learn about obeying.
Then it is easier to obey the next time.

Sweet Thoughts
to Sleep On

God loves you. He is happy to forgive you when you ask Him. He will always give you another chance to obey.

★ Can you name a time when someone forgave you? How about a time when God forgave you?

Dear Father,

Thank You for forgiving me and giving me more and more chances to obey.

Amen.

Being Unselfish

Do not look out only for yourselves.
Look out for the good of others also.
I Corinthians 10:24

When you have brand-new sandbox toys, what do you do?
Do you share them with your friend?
Do you let your friend build things
in the sand with your toys?
Being unselfish means sharing your toys.
It means letting your friends play with them.
Did you know that it feels good to be unselfish?
It feels good to be kind to others
and to share what you have.

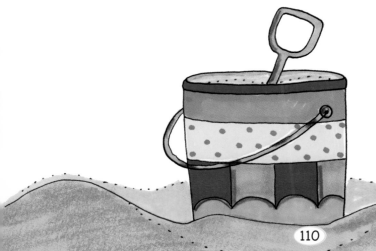

Others will enjoy playing with
you when you are unselfish.
They will learn to be unselfish too —
by your example.

God is pleased when you are unselfish.
It shows that you care about others. He does, too.
Your love for God shines brightly
when you are unselfish!

Sweet Thoughts
to Sleep On

Being unselfish means happily sharing with others.
God is pleased when you share.

★ When did someone unselfishly share with you?

Dear Father,

It isn't always easy to be unselfish.
Please help me to do better and better at it.

Amen.

Praising God

Let everything that breathes praise the LORD.
Psalm 150:6

Yippee, yahoo, hurray for God!
Praising God means telling Him how wonderful He is.
Praise God for giant snow-topped mountains.
Praise Him for big blue oceans.

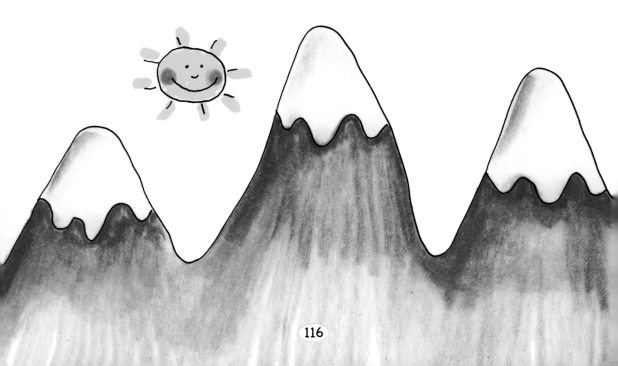

Praise God for puppies that run and play.
Praise Him for moms and dads and grandparents, too.
Praise Him for all your friends.

Praise God for the Bible that teaches us about Him.
Praise Him for everything He does to take care of you.
Praise Him most of all for ... Him!

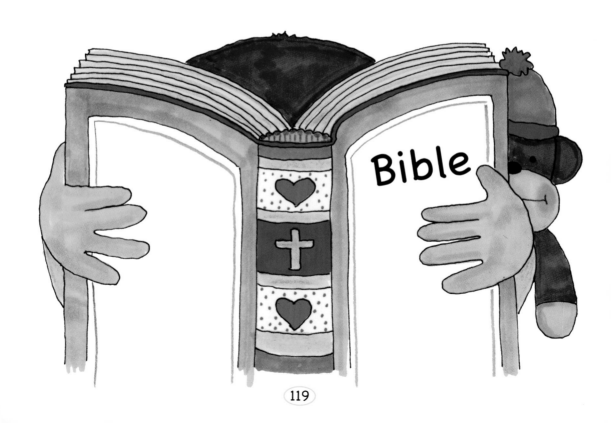

Bible

Sweet Thoughts
to Sleep On

There are a million reasons to praise God. Everything you have and everything around you is a gift from Him!

★ What would you like to praise God for today?

Dear Father,

I do want to praise You! Thank You for everything You give me and for loving me so much!

Amen.

Heaven Is a Wonderful Place!

"Rejoice and be glad, because you have a
great reward waiting for you in heaven."
Matthew 5:12

What do you think about heaven?
Heaven is where God lives!
It is the most amazing place you can dream of.
The Bible says heaven is beautiful.
Do you know something
else about heaven?
God wants you to
come there someday.
God wants you to live
there with Him
someday.

You can come into God's heaven
because of what Jesus did.
He died for your sins, even though He
never did anything wrong Himself.

God brought Him back to life
and now He is in heaven, too.
When you ask Jesus into your heart,
you can know that you will go to God's
wonderful heaven one day.

Sweet Thoughts
to Sleep On

You can know that for sure you will one day go to heaven if you have asked Jesus into your heart.

★ What do you think heaven will be like?

Dear Father,

Thank You for sending Jesus so that I can come to heaven someday. We'll have fun being together forever!

Amen.